BIBLE EXPLO

The Story o Joseph

Leena Lane - Gillian Chapman

Joseph and his brothers

Activity: How many differences can you find between these pictures of Jacob and his sons?

Jacob had a very large family. He had twelve sons and a daughter. He lived with his family in the land of Canaan.

Jacob's sons were called Reuben, Simeon, Levi, Judah, Issachar, Zebulun, Dan, Naphtali, Gad, Asher, Joseph and Benjamin, the youngest son. Out of all his sons, Jacob loved Joseph most of all. Joseph was Jacob's favourite son.

Jacob's sons looked after his sheep and goats. Joseph brought reports to his father about how well or badly his brothers were working. They didn't like it when Joseph told their father they had not been working well!

Genesis 35, verses 23 to 29

Something to think about:
How would you feel if you were one of Joseph's brothers?

Prayer:
Dear God, thank you for my family. Help us to be kind to each other and remember that each one in the family is special.

Joseph's wonderful coat

✏ Activity:
Can you design a colourful coat for Joseph?

When Joseph was seventeen years old, his father Jacob gave him a very special gift. He gave him a wonderful new coat to wear.

Joseph was very proud of his new coat. He strutted around in front of all his brothers, saying, 'Look at me! Look what Dad has bought for me!'

But Joseph's brothers were jealous.

'Why does Dad love Joseph more than us?' they muttered.

'Why haven't we been given robes like that?' they grumbled.

Joseph didn't seem to hear them. He thought only about his handsome coat.

Genesis 37, verses 2 to 4

Something to think about:
Was it fair for Jacob to give only Joseph a special gift?

Prayer:

Dear God, thank you for special gifts I receive from my family and from you. Help me to be grateful for everything I have.

✎ Activity:

Joseph's coat was very colourful. What do you get if you mix the following colours? Fill in the shape with the right colour.

🟡 + 🔵 = ⬜

🔵 + 🔴 = ⬜

🟡 + 🔴 = ⬜

Joseph has strange dreams

One night, Joseph had a very strange dream. He dreamed that he and his brothers were tying up sheaves of corn in a field. Suddenly his sheaf of corn stood up straight and the eleven other sheaves of corn all bowed down to his sheaf.

Joseph's brothers were angry. 'Do you think you will rule over us?' they scoffed.

Another night Joseph dreamed he saw eleven stars, the sun and the moon, all bowing down to him!

Joseph told his father about the dream. Jacob said, 'What is this? Do you think that your mother and I and your brothers will bow down before you?'

Joseph's brothers were very jealous.

Genesis 37, verses 5 to 11

✏️ Activity:
Can you rearrange the letters to discover what Joseph dreamed about?

RATSS

Something to think about:
Do you think Joseph should have kept quiet about his dreams?

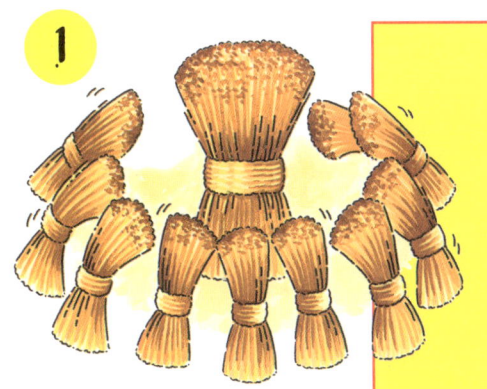

✎ Activity:

Find the two dream pictures that show the same number of sheaves and stars as Joseph had brothers. Put the picture numbers in the boxes below.

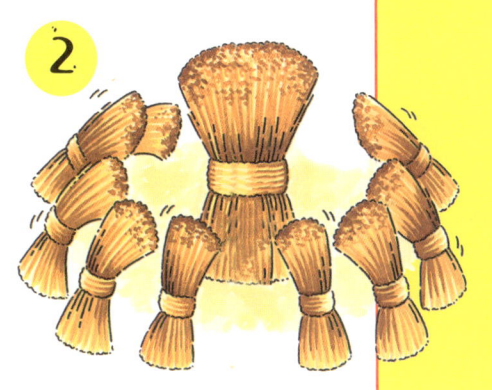

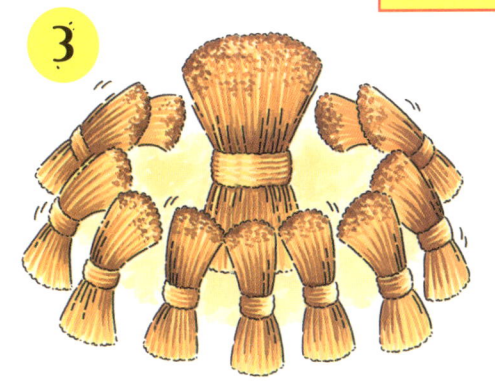

Prayer:

Dear God, help me to think before I speak so that I don't make other people sad.

Joseph's brothers are jealous

Joseph's brothers were very angry with Joseph.

First, he had told their father that they were not working hard enough in the fields with the sheep. Then, their father had given Joseph a fine robe to show that he was their dad's favourite! That made them feel left out.

To make matters even worse, Joseph had started telling them about his strange dreams, in which he was somehow greater than them. They were just old corn stacks and fading stars. Why did Joseph think he was so much more important than them?

The brothers now hated Joseph. They wanted to get rid of him.

Genesis 37, verses 1 to 11

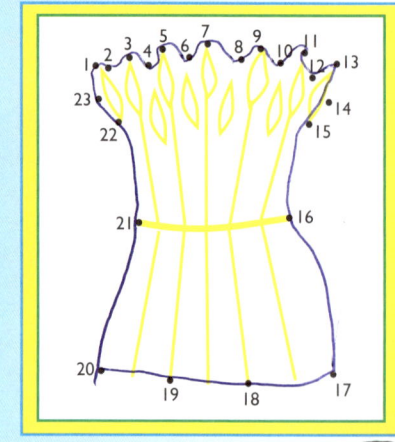

Activity:
Join up the dots to complete this picture.

Something to think about:
Joseph's brothers became so jealous that they hated Joseph. What makes you jealous of other people?

Prayer:
Dear God, I'm sorry for times when I have been jealous of others and when I haven't been kind to them.

Activity:
Which of these are brothers of Joseph? Write yes or no in the boxes.

yes	yes	NO
yes	NO	yes

Joseph is sold to be a slave

One day when the brothers were all out in the fields looking after the sheep, they thought up a cruel plan to get rid of Joseph. 'Let's throw the dreamer into a well and leave him there to die! We'll tell Dad that a wild animal got him,' they plotted.

So when Joseph came to see them, they tore off his fine robe and threw him into an empty well! But a group of travelling traders came past. They were on their way to Egypt. The brothers quickly changed their plan and sold Joseph to the traders. He was taken away as a slave!

The brothers told their father that Joseph had been killed by a wild animal. Jacob tore his clothes and was heartbroken.

Genesis 37, verses 23 to 36

Prayer:
Dear God, please help me to remember that Jesus is always my friend, even if other people are not being friendly.

Something to think about:
Joseph was saved from dying in the well. God had a plan for Joseph's life.

Activity: Can you find six words that describe Joseph's brothers?

```
Q R T A L I A R S F P
W B H S R I B N S S Y
A Y O A N G R Y J S S
  F M D I C R U E L E
      T O     R A Y L
              H L M F
              G O E I
              D U S S
              R S H H
              E Z A P
              E I P L
```

Joseph works for Potiphar

Joseph was taken to Egypt, where he was sold as a slave to Potiphar, the captain of the palace guard. God looked after Joseph.

Joseph worked hard in Potiphar's home and everyone liked him. Potiphar put Joseph in charge of his household. God blessed Potiphar's household when Joseph was in charge. God helped Joseph to do well at his job.

One day, things changed. Potiphar's wife told lies about Joseph and said he had tried to hurt her. Potiphar was furious and threw Joseph into jail. But God was with Joseph there too. Joseph had done nothing wrong.

Genesis 39, verses 1 to 21

Something to think about:
God helped Joseph to do well at his work. God blessed the people around him.

Prayer:

Dear God, when things don't go quite as I expect, please help me to trust you. Thank you that you are always with me.

✏ Activity:

Only six of the picture details below were taken from the pictures on this page. Can you mark them with a tick, and put a cross next to the two that don't come from this page?

Joseph in jail

Joseph was thrown into jail where the king's prisoners were kept. But very soon the warden of the jail began to like Joseph. He gave him jobs to do. Joseph did well because God was helping him.

It wasn't long before the warden decided to put Joseph in charge of the other prisoners. The warden trusted him.

In jail, Joseph met the king's chief baker and the king's wine steward. One night they both had very strange dreams which troubled them. They asked Joseph to help them.

Genesis 39, verses 19 to 23; chapter 40, verses 1 to 23

Something to think about:
God was always with Joseph, even in jail when he didn't know if he'd ever be free again.

✏ Activity:
Which prisoner was the king's baker, which one was the wine steward and which one was a shepherd? You can write the answers above each prisoner.

Baker

15

Sheperd   Steward

Prayer:
Dear God, please be with people in jail, especially those who have done nothing wrong, or who are in jail for being Christians.

Joseph understands dreams

Joseph asked the wine steward and the baker to tell him their dreams.

The wine steward spoke first: 'I saw a grapevine with three branches. The grapes became ripe and I squeezed them into the king's cup and gave it to him to drink.' Joseph told him that in three days he would be freed from jail.

The baker spoke next, but his dream did not end happily. 'I was carrying three baskets of cakes and pastries, when some birds swooped down and ate them all up!' said the baker.

Joseph looked sad. 'I'm sorry to say you will never be free. The king means to kill you in three days!'

Three days later, the dreams came true, just as Joseph had said!

Genesis 40, verses 1 to 23

Something to think about:
God helped Joseph to understand dreams. Can you think of anyone else in the Bible who had strange dreams?

Prayer:

Dear God, please be with me in my dreams and through each night.

✏ Activity:

To re-create this picture the squares have to be put in the correct place, Can you put the correct position number in each circle?

Pharaoh's dreams

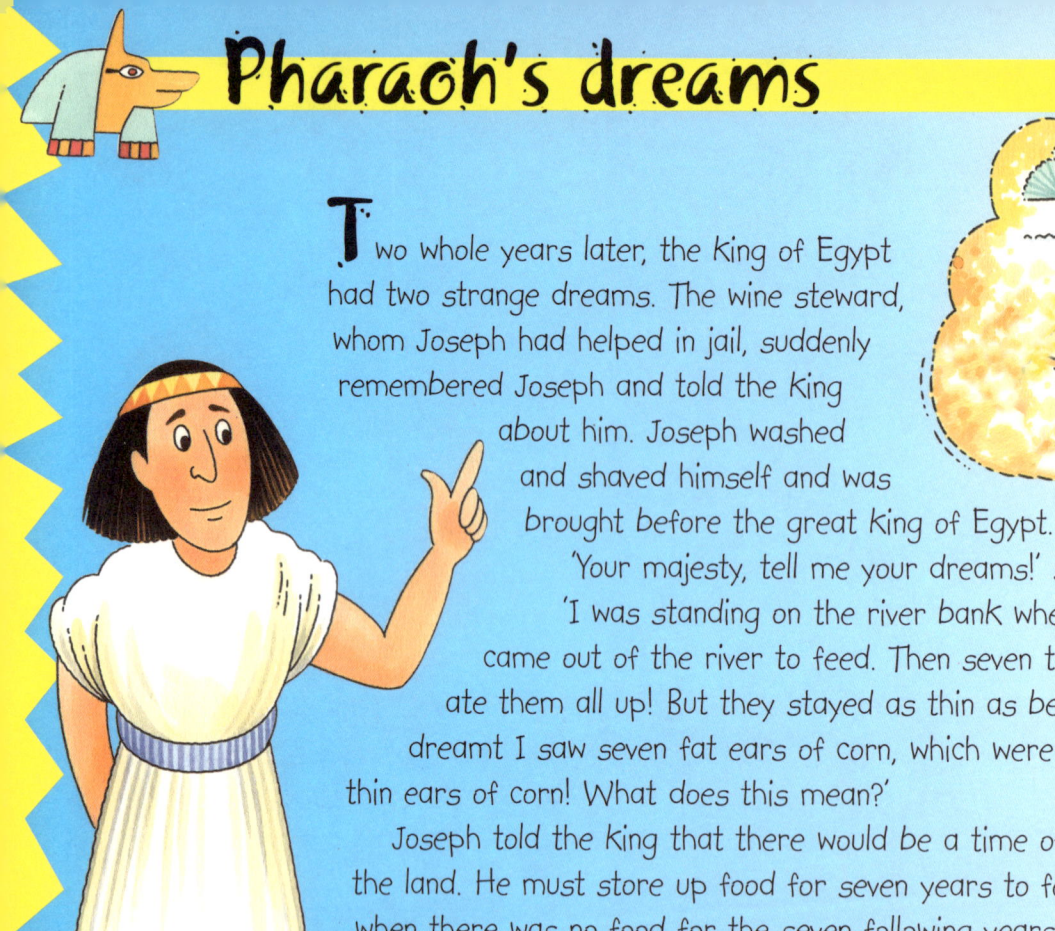

Two whole years later, the King of Egypt had two strange dreams. The wine steward, whom Joseph had helped in jail, suddenly remembered Joseph and told the King about him. Joseph washed and shaved himself and was brought before the great king of Egypt.

'Your majesty, tell me your dreams!' said Joseph.

'I was standing on the river bank when seven fat cows came out of the river to feed. Then seven thin cows came and ate them all up! But they stayed as thin as before! Then I dreamt I saw seven fat ears of corn, which were eaten up by seven thin ears of corn! What does this mean?'

Joseph told the king that there would be a time of great famine in the land. He must store up food for seven years to feed the people when there was no food for the seven following years.

The King was delighted and put Joseph in charge of storing food for Egypt.

Genesis 41, verses 1 to 43

Something to think about:
Joseph went from being a prisoner to being the King's special governor. What a turnaround!

✏️ Activity:

The King counted the cows in his dream. Can you find the answers to these strange sums?

◯ =1   ╱ =2   ∽ =3

〰 =4   ▯ =5   ▮ =6

👁 =7   ◓ =8   ⬤ =9

◯ + 〰 = ☐

◓ − 👁 + ╱ = ☐

⬤ + ∽ − ▮ = ☐

You could write your answers with numbers or draw the *symbol* that represents the answer.

Prayer: Dear God, thank you that you have a plan for my life too.

Joseph sees his brothers again

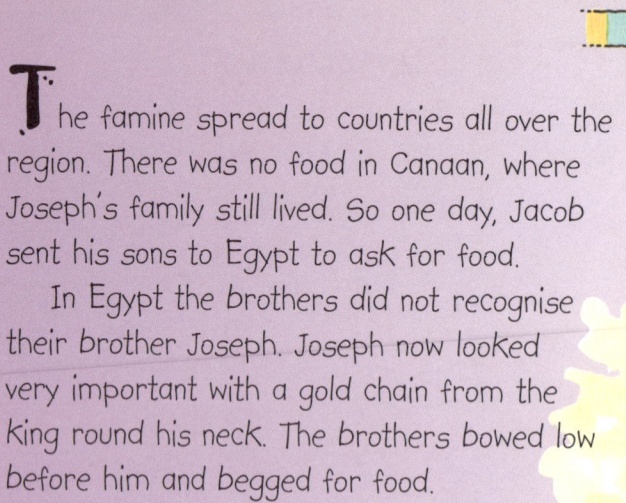

The famine spread to countries all over the region. There was no food in Canaan, where Joseph's family still lived. So one day, Jacob sent his sons to Egypt to ask for food.

In Egypt the brothers did not recognise their brother Joseph. Joseph now looked very important with a gold chain from the King round his neck. The brothers bowed low before him and begged for food.

At first, Joseph wanted to test them to see whether they had changed their ways. He saw that they were very sorry for what they had done. Eventually he told them who he was. They were frightened in case he was still angry, but Joseph forgave them.

Genesis 42 to 45

Prayer: Dear God, help me to forgive people when they say sorry, just as you forgive me.

Activity:

You can colour in this picture of Joseph. Would Joseph's brothers recognise him from your picture?

Something to think about:

Joseph's brothers bowed down to him. Can you remember what Joseph had seen in his dreams?

Joseph sees his father again

Joseph sent his brothers back to Canaan to fetch Jacob, their father.

'Joseph is alive! He's in Egypt!' they told him excitedly. 'In fact, he is ruler of Egypt!' Jacob could hardly believe it. His beloved son was alive!

Joseph had sent carts to bring Jacob and their family back to Egypt.

God spoke to Jacob in a dream, telling him not to be afraid to go to Egypt. 'I will go with you,' promised God.

So Jacob made the journey and Joseph came out to meet him. He threw his arms around his father's neck and wept tears of joy.

Jacob stayed in Egypt with Joseph to the end of his days. The king allowed them all to live in the land and Joseph made sure they always had enough food. God blessed Joseph's family.

Genesis 46 to 47, verse 12

✏️ Activity:
Can you help Jacob to find the way to Joseph?

Something to think about:
Jacob thought he would never see Joseph again. But God surprised him!

Prayer:
Dear God, thank you for all that you give us, and that you sometimes give us lovely surprises too!

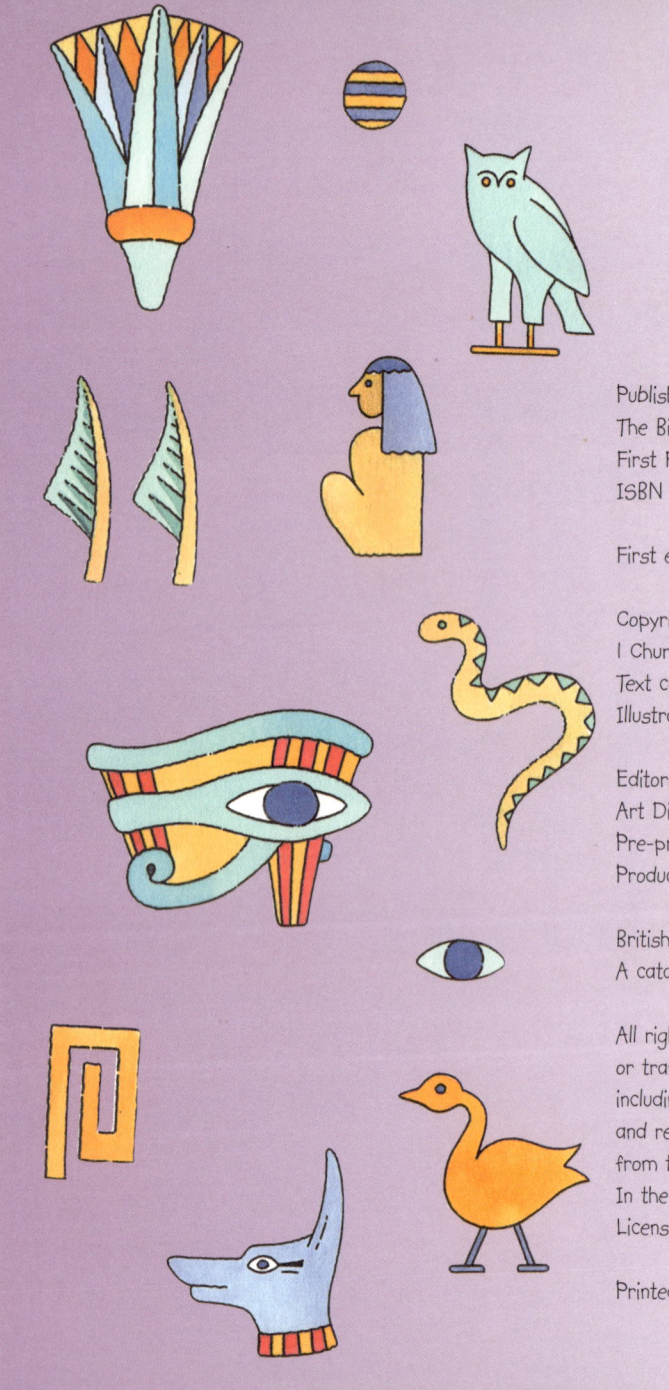

Published in the UK by
The Bible Reading Fellowship
First Floor, Elsfield Hall, 15-17 Elsfield Way, Oxford OX2 8FG
ISBN 1 84101 451 6

First edition 2005

Copyright © 2005 AD Publishing Services Ltd
1 Churchgates, The Wilderness, Berkhamsted, Herts HP4 2UB
Text copyright © 2005 AD Publishing Services Ltd, Leena Lane
Illustrations copyright © 2005 Gillian Chapman

Editorial Director Annette Reynolds
Art Director Gerald Rogers
Pre-production Krystyna Hewitt
Production John Laister

British Library Cataloguing in Publication Data.
A catalogue record for this book is available from the British Library.

All rights reserved. No part of this publication may be reproduced or transmitted in any form or by any means, electronic or mechanical, including photocopying, recording or any information storage and retrieval system, without either prior permission in writing from the publisher or a licence permitting restricted copying. In the United Kingdom such licences are issued by the Publishers Licensing Society Ltd, 90 Tottenham Court Road, London W1P 9HE.

Printed and bound in Singapore